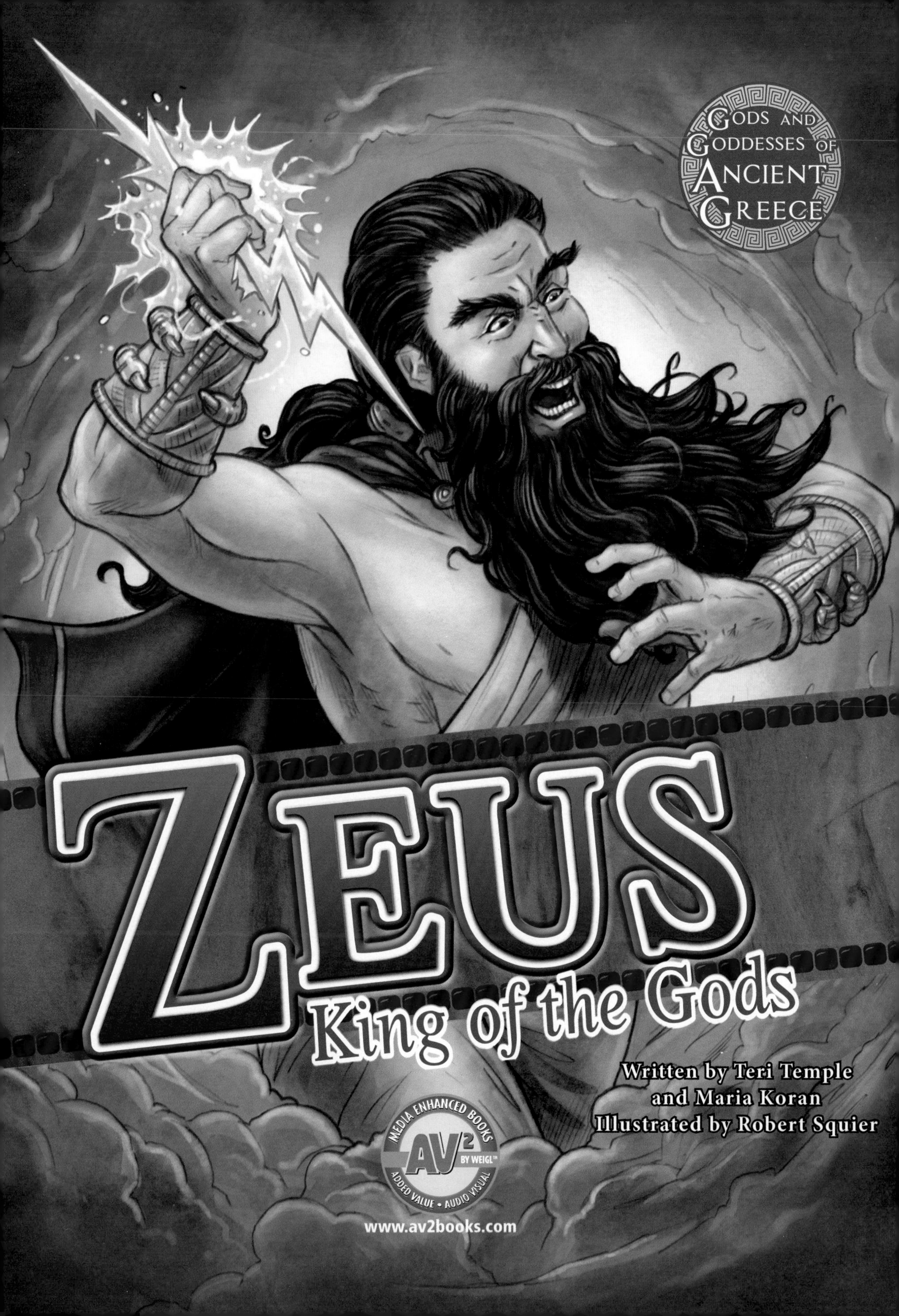

GODS AND GODDESSES OF ANCIENT GREECE

ZEUS
King of the Gods

Written by Teri Temple
and Maria Koran
Illustrated by Robert Squier

MEDIA ENHANCED BOOKS
AV²
BY WEIGL™
ADDED VALUE · AUDIO VISUAL

www.av2books.com

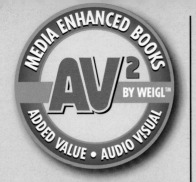

AV² provides enriched content that supplements and complements this book. Weigl's AV² books strive to create inspired learning and engage young minds in a total learning experience.

Your AV² Media Enhanced books come alive with...

Audio
Listen to sections of the book read aloud.

Key Words
Study vocabulary, and complete a matching word activity.

Video
Watch informative video clips.

Quizzes
Test your knowledge.

Embedded Weblinks
Gain additional information for research.

Slide Show
View images and captions, and prepare a presentation.

Try This!
Complete activities and hands-on experiments.

... and much, much more!

Go to **www.av2books.com**, and enter this book's unique code.

BOOK CODE

M 299223

AV² by Weigl brings you media enhanced books that support active learning.

Published by AV² by Weigl
350 5th Avenue, 59th Floor
New York, NY 10118
Website: www.av2books.com

Printed in Brainerd, Minnesota, United States
1 2 3 4 5 6 7 8 9 0 20 19 18 17 16

072016
070416

Project Coordinator: Warren Rylands
Art Director: Terry Paulhus

Every reasonable effort has been made to trace ownership and to obtain permission to reprint copyright material. The publishers would be pleased to have any errors or omissions brought to their attention so that they may be corrected in subsequent printings.

Weigl acknowledges iStock as its primary image supplier for this title.

Library of Congress Cataloging-in-Publication Data

Names: Temple, Teri, author.
Title: Zeus / Teri Temple.
Description: New York : AV² by Weigl, 2016. | Series: Gods and goddesses of ancient Greece | Includes index.
Identifiers: LCCN 2016002892 (print) | LCCN 2016004277 (ebook) | ISBN 9781489646538 (hard cover : alk. paper) | ISBN 9781489650474 (soft cover : alk. paper) | ISBN 9781489646545 (Multi-User eBook)
Subjects: LCSH: Zeus (Greek deity)--Juvenile literature. | Mythology, Greek--Juvenile literature. | Gods, Greek--Juvenile literature.
Classification: LCC BL820.J8 T46 2016 (print) | LCC BL820.J8 (ebook) | DDC 292.2/113--dc23
LC record available at http://lccn.loc.gov/2016002892

CONTENTS

2 AV² Book Code

4 Introduction

6 Characters and Places

8 The King of the Gods

30 Principal Gods
of Greek Mythology—
A Family Tree

31 Key Words/Index

32 Log on to
www.av2books.com

ZEUS 3

INTRODUCTION

L ong ago in **ancient Greece** and Rome, most people believed that gods and goddesses ruled their world. Storytellers shared the adventures of these gods to help explain all the mysteries in life. The gods were immortal, meaning they lived forever. Their stories were full of love and tragedy, fearsome monsters, brave heroes, and struggles for power. The storytellers wove aspects of Greek customs and beliefs into the tales. Some stories told of the creation of the world and the origins of the gods. Others helped explain natural events such as earthquakes and storms. People believed the tales, which over time became myths.

The ancient Greeks and Romans **worshiped** the gods by building temples and statues in their honor. They felt the gods would protect and guide them. People passed down the myths through the generations by word of mouth. Later, famous poets such as Homer and Hesiod wrote them down. Today, these myths give us a unique look at what life was like in ancient Greece more than 2,000 years ago.

ANCIENT GREEK SOCIETIES

In ancient Greece, cities, towns, and their surrounding farmlands were called city-states. These city-states each had their own governments. They made their own laws. The individual city-states were very independent. They never joined to become one whole nation. They did, however, share a common language, religion, and culture.

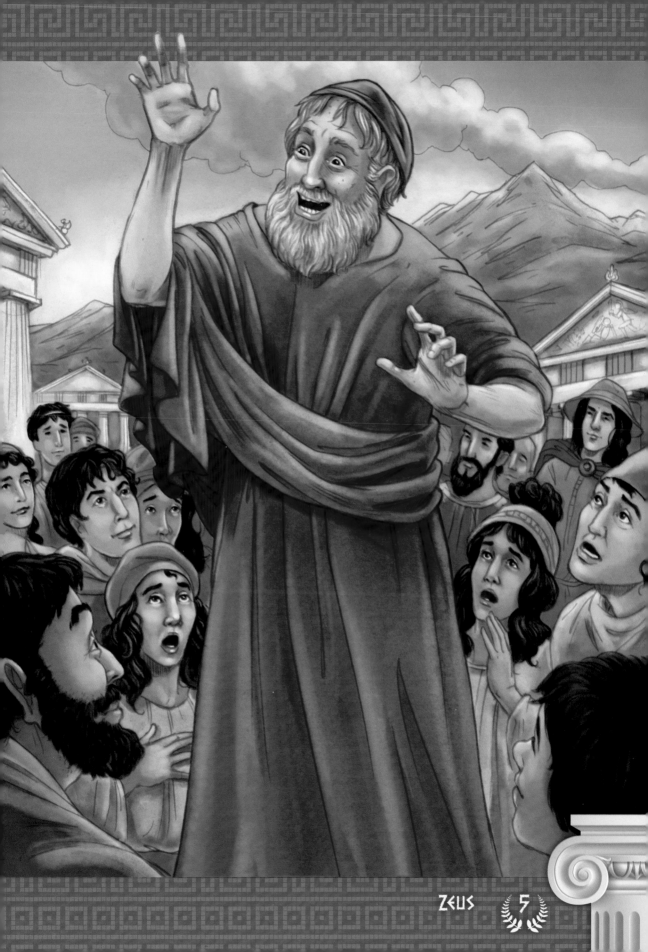

ZEUS 5

CHARACTERS AND PLACES

Mount Olympus
The mountaintop home of the 12 Olympic gods

Aegean Sea

Olympia, Greece
The home of the first Olympic Games founded and held every four years in honor of Zeus

Mount Ida, Island of Crete
Birthplace of Zeus

ANCIENT GREECE

CRETE

Olympian Gods
Demeter, Hermes, Hephaestus, Aphrodite, Ares, Hera, Zeus, Poseidon, Athena, Apollo, Artemis, and Dionysus

Tartarus (TAHR-tuh-rus)
The lowest region of the world, part of the underworld; a prison for the defeated Titans and gods; one of the ancient gods

Chaos (KAY-ahs)
The formless darkness that existed at the beginning of time

Titans
The 12 children of Gaea and Cronus; god-like giants that are said to represent the forces of nature

Cronus (CROW-nus)
A Titan who ruled the world; married to Rhea and their children became the first six Olympic gods

Cyclopes (SIGH-clopes)
One-eyed giants; children of Gaea and Uranus

Gaea (JEE-uh)
Mother Earth and one of the first elements born to Chaos; mother of the Titans, Cyclopes and Hecatoncheires

Hecatoncheires (hek-a-TON-kear-eez)
Monstrous creatures with 100 arms and 50 heads; children of Gaea and Uranus

Rhea (RAY-UH)
A Titaness; married to her brother Cronus; mother to the first six Olympic gods: Zeus, Poseidon, Hades, Demeter, Hestia, and Hera

Typhon (TIE-fon)
Monster created by Gaea to fight Zeus

Uranus (YOO-ruh-nus)
The Sky and Heavens; born of Gaea along with the mountains and seas; husband of Gaea; father of the Titans, Cyclopes, and Hecatoncheires

Zeus (ZOO-S)
Supreme ruler of the heavens and weather and of the gods who lived on Mount Olympus; youngest son of Cronus and Rhea; married to Hera; father of many gods and heroes

THE KING OF THE GODS

In the beginning there was only darkness and confusion. It was known as Chaos. Order grew in the darkness. Out of it came Gaea, or Mother Earth. She was the mother of all living things. She gave birth to the heavens and sky and named them Uranus.

Together Gaea and Uranus ruled over the world and had many children. Their first 12 children were wondrous and beautiful giants known as the Titans. They represented the forces of nature.

Later Gaea and Uranus added more children to their family. Three were called the Cyclopes and three known as the Hecatoncheires. The Cyclopes were mighty one-eyed giants. The Hecatoncheires were monsters. Each had 100 arms and 50 heads.

Uranus hated these monstrous children because they were ugly. He worried the Titans might try to steal his power. So he imprisoned them all in Tartarus. This made Gaea angry. She tried to convince the Titans to rebel against their father.

Only the youngest was brave enough to try. With an unbreakable **sickle** from his mother, Cronus defeated his father. As the new ruler of the universe, Cronus and his wife Rhea gave birth to the first gods. Zeus would be their youngest.

ZEUS

Cronus worried that his children would try to overthrow him, just as he had done to his father. So after each child was born, he swallowed it up. This made Rhea very sad and lonely. Finally, when she was expecting their sixth child, she decided to trick Cronus.

When the baby boy arrived, Rhea hid him in a cave near Mount Ida on the island of **Crete**. She then returned to Cronus. She wrapped a stone in a blanket and gave it to Cronus as their child. He thought it was the baby and swallowed the stone. Meanwhile, baby Zeus stayed hidden away on the island. He grew and prospered, cared for by woodland nymphs and a she-goat named Amalthaea, who fed him her milk. When Zeus cried, guards would clash their weapons together to hide the sound. When Zeus was an adult, he returned to face his father.

CAPRICORN CONSTELLATION

Capricorn, also called the goat, is the tenth sign of the **zodiac**. The legend is that Zeus gave Amalthaea a horn that was always full of food. This gave us the expression "Horn of Plenty." At her death, Zeus set her image among the stars as the star Capella in the constellation of Capricorn. Then he made an impenetrable breastplate, the Aegis, from her hide.

Zeus learned of his father's evil deeds from his mother and vowed to dethrone him. He took as his first wife Metis, a Titan's daughter. Metis was the goddess of prudence and was very wise. She knew Cronus had the Titans on his side. They needed to devise a plan to find help for Zeus. Rhea, his mother, discovered a way.

Metis gave Cronus a drink by tricking him into thinking it would make him unbeatable. Instead it made him throw up, first the stone and then his children, all in one piece! Zeus now had three sisters, Hestia, Demeter, and Hera, and two brothers, Poseidon and Hades. They were overjoyed at being released. They enthusiastically joined Zeus in his quest.

But Zeus knew more help was needed to win a battle against the Titans. His grandmother Gaea told him he could gain powerful allies if he released her children from the underworld. So he journeyed to Tartarus to free his uncles, the Cyclopes and the Hecatoncheires.

Great blacksmiths and builders, the Cyclopes created weapons for the upcoming battle. Their gift to Zeus was his thunderbolt. With it, he could shake the universe. For Poseidon they fashioned a trident, a three-pronged spear that could divide the seas.

FOOD OF THE GODS

The gods and goddesses were immortals. They had a divine ichor flowing in their veins instead of blood. This allowed them to live forever. This blessing came from their food and drink, ambrosia and nectar. Some myths say it comes from an edible flowerlike plant. Legend has it that anyone who eats ambrosia will live forever.

Lastly for Hades they created a helmet of darkness that allowed him to move invisibly among his enemies. Zeus and his allies were now ready to face Cronus in battle.

Each side prepared for battle. The Titans gathered at Mount Othrys, led by Atlas. The children of Cronus made their way to Mount Olympus and a huge battle began. While not gods, the Titans were giant creatures of unbelievable strength. Zeus and his siblings were just as strong, however. And they had the Cyclopes and the Hecatoncheires as their allies.

The war raged for ten long years. The weapons the Cyclopes made ultimately gave Zeus the advantage. First they used the helmet of darkness to sneak into the Titans' camp. Then they stole all of Cronus's weapons. Poseidon's trident was then used as a diversion while Zeus hit the Titans with his thunderbolts. The crushing blow came as the Cyclopes and Hecatoncheires battered the Titans with boulders.

TYPHON AND VOLCANOES

Mother Earth was angry with Zeus for sending her children, the Titans, to Tartarus. So she created two horrible monsters, Typhon and his mate Echidna. She set them on the gods, who were so frightened they transformed themselves into animals and fled. Impossibly large, Typhon had 100 heads. His eyes dripped venom and his mouth spewed lava. Roaring like 100 lions, he tore up whole mountains. Zeus found the courage to face him. He used his thunderbolts to bury him under Mount Etna. Legend says that Typhon is trapped there to this day. His smoke and lava erupt out of the mountaintop.

With their fort weakened and the universe nearly destroyed, the Titans gave up the fight. Zeus had Cronus and his troops imprisoned in Tartarus. The Hecatoncheires guarded against their escape.

Peace fell upon Earth. The brothers decided to draw lots to see who would be the king of the gods. To draw lots is to pick an object that represents a choice. When you pick, your decision is based on chance. Zeus drew the best lot. He became the ruler of the universe and king of the gods. Hades was made god of the underworld. Poseidon was made god of the sea.

Hephaestus, the god of fire, built a palace worthy of the gods with the help of the Cyclopes. High atop the summit of Mount Olympus, hidden behind snow and clouds, was the magnificent home of the 12 Olympic gods and goddesses. They ruled over the heavens and protected Earth.

Zeus lived on Mount Olympus. At his side were Poseidon, Hephaestus, and his sister Demeter, goddess of the harvest, with her daughter Persephone. Next came Aphrodite, goddess of love, and her son Eros, better known as Cupid. The rest were children of Zeus: Ares, the god of war; Hermes, the messenger god; the twins Apollo and Artemis, god and goddess of the sun and moon; Dionysus, god of wine; and Athena, goddess of wisdom. Zeus's gentle sister Hestia tended the hearth for the gods. And Hades preferred his realm far below in the underworld.

OLYMPIC GAMES

Olympia, Greece, was also the birthplace of the first Olympic games. The Olympic Games began as a festival that was celebrated every four years in honor of Zeus. The people who came prayed and made sacrifices to Zeus for success and luck in their lives. The very first Olympics, in 776 BC, had just one footrace in it. Records show that the first Olympic champion was a lowly cook by the name of Coroebus of Elis. The festivities concluded with a special sacrifice of 100 cattle to Zeus.

Zeus was an imposing leader, tall and strong. He was able to change his shape as easily as the weather he controlled. He was often seen as a handsome bearded man with a thunderbolt in his hand and an eagle at his side. He was the god who upheld the laws of the people. Wise and fair, he could be cruel in his punishments to those who broke these laws. He loved the people on Earth and was the protector of the innocent, offering them guidance and praise.

Zeus had to keep peace on Mount Olympus. The gods were always up to something. Their **quarrels** and battles could be heard below on Earth. But Zeus was not so innocent himself. He often created mischief in his adventures.

THUNDER AND LIGHTNING

Ancient Greeks believed that many things we now explain with science were the result of gods. They believed that thunder was the result of angering Zeus. The lightning bolts were thought to be his way of punishing humans. They also believed thunder was the quarreling gods high on Mount Olympus. Ancient Greeks tried very hard not to anger Zeus or his fellow gods.

Zeus liked to check on the people of Earth. And he often fell in love with the beautiful maidens he encountered. Europa was one such woman. She was the daughter of Agenor, king of Phoenicia. Zeus noticed her from the heavens and immediately became enchanted. He changed himself into a magnificent white bull and went down to greet her. Europa was at first afraid, but Zeus, disguised as the bull, lay gently at her feet. As she grew braver, she petted the bull. Then she climbed on its back. That was all it took. Zeus carried her off over the ocean to the island of Crete.

Another unsuspecting maiden was Leda, wife of the king of Sparta. This time, Zeus changed into a swan. Pretending that an eagle was attacking him, the swan dove into Leda's arms for protection. Zeus was forever trying to win the hearts of women and goddesses. It was from these love affairs that many of the heroes and beauties of ancient Greece were born. Among them were Heracles, Helen of Troy, Perseus, and Persephone.

WOMEN'S ROLES IN ANCIENT GREECE

Ancient Greek society had different levels. Some citizens were wealthy and others were extremely poor. Some were even slaves. Men and women did not share the same rights. Women were considered less important. They could not hold jobs or help run the government. Wealthy women spent their days getting pampered by slaves and preparing for parties. Lower-class women spent their days doing chores, working in fields, and caring for children.

Zeus chose the lovely Hera to be his final wife. She was the goddess of marriage and queen of the gods. When she and Zeus wed, all of nature burst forth in bloom. Zeus believed that the more wives he had, the more children he would receive. Since all of his children would inherit some of his power, they would go on to become heroes, rulers, and even gods themselves.

Everyone should have been happy, but Hera was a jealous wife. She was prone to fits of **rage** when Zeus spent time with other wives and maidens. Hera kept a close eye on Zeus. Despite being the most powerful of gods, Zeus was afraid of Hera's anger. He often tried to sneak behind her back.

Together they had three powerful children. Ares, the god of war, was a troublesome boy and his parents were not very fond of him. Next came gentle Hebe, goddess of youth. She became a cupbearer to the gods on Mount Olympus. Their last son was the deformed and ugly god of fire, Hephaestus. Hera claimed to have had him on her own because she was angry with Zeus over the birth of Athena. Athena had sprung fully formed from Zeus's forehead, dressed in full armor. Athena was Zeus's favorite. He trusted her to carry his thunderbolt and gave her his breastplate, the Aegis. Zeus didn't forget his wish for more children, though. He had courted many lovers before his marriage to Hera.

One of Zeus's most prominent symbols was the eagle, which appeared on many ancient Greek coins.

One who had caught Zeus's eye was Maia. She was the eldest and most beautiful daughter of the Titan Atlas. Together, Zeus and Maia had Hermes, who would become the messenger to the gods. Zeus also fell in love with Demeter, his eldest sister. They had a daughter, Persephone, who would one day rule the underworld with Hades.

Many of Zeus's partners did not escape Hera's watchful eye. The jealous newlywed Hera set a giant snake after Leto, who was pregnant with Zeus's twins. Leto barely escaped. Hera ordered all of the lands in the world to refuse Leto shelter. When Leto was ready to deliver her babies, no one would give her shelter. They were all afraid of Hera's vengeful anger. There was still hope. Poseidon, the god of the sea, had just created a new island. It was floating on the water. He had not yet anchored it down. It was the island of Delos. On the island, Leto finally gave birth to her babies. First came Artemis. She was as lovely as the moon. Artemis would become the goddess of the hunt and protector of all newborn creatures. Then came her twin brother Apollo. He was as glorious as the Sun, fair haired and bright. Apollo would become the god of the Sun. Zeus was proud of all of his children but tried to stay out of the quarrels that erupted between Hera and the other mothers.

Zeus was kept busy ruling the lands. He often dealt out punishments to **offenders**. Prometheus was one who got on Zeus's bad side.

Prometheus felt sorry for the people on Earth because they were cold and lived in the dark. So he decided to steal fire from the sacred hearth on Mount Olympus. After delivering the embers, he made the ancient Greeks promise to never let the Olympic fires go out. In gratitude, they burned sacrifices to the gods. Zeus smelled the sacrifices and was furious that someone had stolen their fire.

ZEUS'S TEMPLE

One temple dedicated to Zeus surpassed them all. It was home to the Statue of Zeus by the sculptor **Phidias**. Located in Olympia, it would become one of the Seven Wonders of the Ancient World. It no longer exists today.

But Prometheus wasn't finished with his mischief yet. He showed the humans how to wrap up only the scraps and bones in the fat of the animals to offer as sacrifice. This allowed them to save the best portions of the meat for themselves. Zeus was beside himself with anger. Not only had Prometheus stolen fire from the gods, he had taught the people how to cheat them as well.

For this crime, Zeus had Prometheus chained in unbreakable links to the top of the mountain. Every day an eagle would attack him and eat his liver. Every night it would grow back because he was an immortal. People quickly learned it was not smart to anger the gods.

Zeus was a favorite subject of the ancient storytellers. As they traveled around they **embellished** his stories and combined them with other stories they heard. He ended up with many wives, children, and legendary adventures. Despite being the most powerful of the gods, he was not the most worshipped. The ancient Greeks were not always happy with the stories they heard. But they believed that the gods and goddesses influenced their lives, so they worked to keep all of them happy. The amazing and entertaining stories of Zeus are sure to inspire generations of writers, artists, and believers to come.

Zeus is often compared to Jupiter, the chief ancient Roman god. Jupiter was also a sky god who was believed to control the weather.

PRINCIPAL GODS OF GREEK MYTHOLOGY— A FAMILY TREE

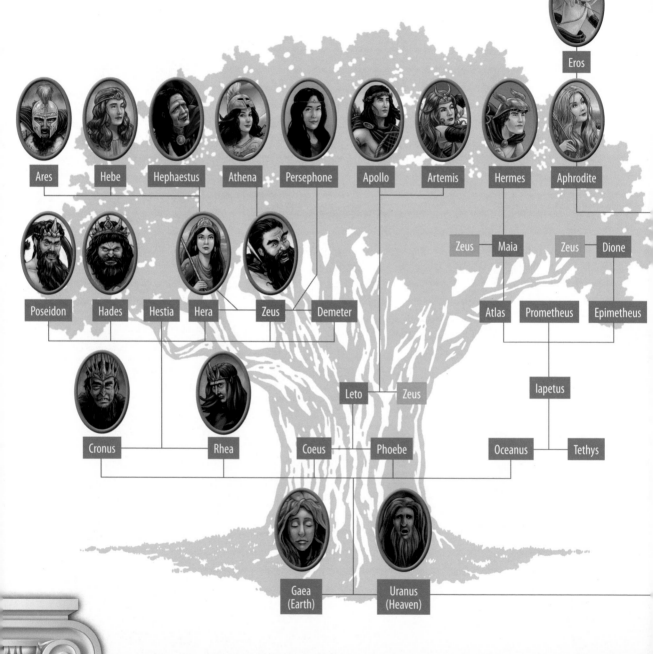

Eros

Ares Hebe Hephaestus Athena Persephone Apollo Artemis Hermes Aphrodite

Zeus Maia Zeus Dione

Poseidon Hades Hestia Hera Zeus Demeter Atlas Prometheus Epimetheus

Iapetus

Cronus Rhea Leto Zeus Coeus Phoebe Oceanus Tethys

Gaea (Earth) Uranus (Heaven)

KEY WORDS

ancient Greece: historical period that lasted from about 800 to 323 BC, during which many advancements were made in politics, art, philosophy, and science

Crete: the largest island that forms part of modern Greece, located in the eastern Mediterranean Sea

embellished: enhancing a story with details that make it more interesting or appealing, but may not be true

offenders: those who break a law or rule

Phidias: a famous Athenian sculptor. It is said that only he saw the exact image of the gods, and he revealed it to man

quarrels: noisy disputes or arguments

rage: violent and extreme anger that is difficult to control

sickle: a tool with a short handle and a sharp, curved metal blade that is usually used for cutting grass or grains

worshiped: showed respect and honor, often through prayer or other religious acts

zodiac: imaginary area in the sky that the planets, Sun, and Moon appear to travel through. The zodiac is divided into 12 parts that each have a special name and symbol, believed by some people to influence events

INDEX

Aegis 10, 23
Aphrodite 6, 17, 30
Apollo 6, 17, 25, 30
Ares 6, 17, 23, 30
Artemis 6, 17, 25, 30
Athena 6, 17, 23, 30

Cronus 6, 7, 8, 10, 13, 14, 16, 30
Cyclopes 7, 8, 13, 14, 17

Demeter 6, 7, 13, 17, 25, 30
Dionysus 6, 17

Eros 17, 30

Gaea 6, 7, 8, 13, 30

Hades 7, 13, 14, 16, 17, 25, 30
Hecatoncheires 7, 8, 13, 14, 16
Hephaestus 6, 17, 23, 30
Hera 6, 7, 13, 20, 23, 25, 30
Hermes 6, 17, 25, 30
Hestia 7, 13, 17, 30

Mount Olympus 6, 7, 14, 17, 18, 23, 26

Olympia, Greece 6, 17, 26
Olympic games 6, 17

Persephone 17, 20, 25, 30
Poseidon 6, 7, 13, 14, 16, 17, 25, 30

Titans 6, 7, 8, 13, 14, 16

Uranus 7, 8, 30

Log on to www.av2books.com

AV² by Weigl brings you media enhanced books that support active learning. Go to www.av2books.com, and enter the special code found on page 2 of this book. You will gain access to enriched and enhanced content that supplements and complements this book. Content includes video, audio, weblinks, quizzes, a slide show, and activities.

AV² Online Navigation

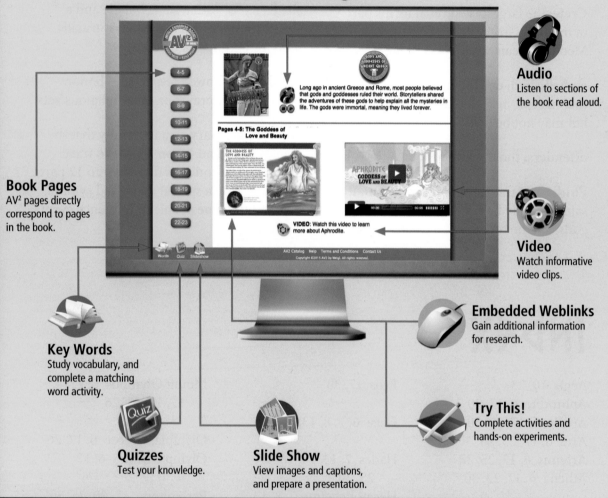

Audio
Listen to sections of the book read aloud.

Book Pages
AV² pages directly correspond to pages in the book.

Video
Watch informative video clips.

Key Words
Study vocabulary, and complete a matching word activity.

Embedded Weblinks
Gain additional information for research.

Quizzes
Test your knowledge.

Slide Show
View images and captions, and prepare a presentation.

Try This!
Complete activities and hands-on experiments.

AV² was built to bridge the gap between print and digital. We encourage you to tell us what you like and what you want to see in the future.

Sign up to be an AV² Ambassador at www.av2books.com/ambassador.

Due to the dynamic nature of the Internet, some of the URLs and activities provided as part of AV² by Weigl may have changed or ceased to exist. AV² by Weigl accepts no responsibility for any such changes. All media enhanced books are regularly monitored to update addresses and sites in a timely manner. Contact AV² by Weigl at 1-866-649-3445 or av2books@weigl.com with any questions, comments, or feedback.